My Diary of Hope, Despair & Freedom

Motivational, Emancipation & Educational

Cecilia Naa Densua Quarshie

My Diary Poetry of Hope, Despair & Freedom

My Diary Poetry of Hope, Despair & Freedom

Motivational, Emancipation & Educational

Cecilia Naa Densua Quarshie

authorHOUSE®

AuthorHouse™
1663 Liberty Drive
Bloomington, IN 47403
www.authorhouse.com
Phone: 1-800-839-8640

First published by AuthorHouse   08/30/2011

ISBN: 978-1-4567-9732-4 (sc)
ISBN: 978-1-4567-9733-1 (ebk)

Printed in the United States of America

Any people depicted in stock imagery provided by Thinkstock are models, and such images are being used for illustrative purposes only.
Certain stock imagery © Thinkstock.

This book is printed on acid-free paper.

Because of the dynamic nature of the Internet, any web addresses or links contained in this book may have changed since publication and may no longer be valid. The views expressed in this work are solely those of the author and do not necessarily reflect the views of the publisher, and the publisher hereby disclaims any responsibility for them.

To contact the author please write to
ceciliaghfin@yahoo.co.uk

Contents

Preface

This book is made for all individuals who may be in different emotional states from time to time in their daily lives. It serves as a therapy in soothing wounded wounds, negative thoughts and unfortunate experiences in life. The poems have been divided into different sections where some are religious base; few address educational issues and others are on emancipation or the struggle of the oppressed. The poems on religious backings are much focused in the Christian religious ways where a few references are made from the Bible. The motivational section is mainly to serve as a therapy to people who fall victims of different emotional states in life like bitterness, un-forgiveness, giving up, marriage, true love and so on.

For classroom purposes such as discussions, the writer uses a number of literary features in some of the poems. Some of the poems are clear and straightforward whereas others are not straightforward. Some get the interest of the reader going as this keeps the reader in suspense and anxious for what follows next.

It is the writers hope that all readers make good use of the book in their own unique ways.

Acknowledgments

I wish to thank Michael Duodu an I.T consultant in the United States for the encouragements he gave me many years ago in coming up with my own poetry book.

The following were very helpful in encouraging me towards the completion of the book: Bryden Nii Laryea Koney, David Ebo Arthur, my godfather Emmanuel Boadi, Monitoring and Evaluation Specialist, UNDP, Harare-Zimbabwe and also Doctor Robert Kwesi Mensah Reproductive Health Specialist, UNFPA,Ghana.

Kitari Mayele, cultural producer of Caisa, Finland, I have not forgotten you, thank you as well for the encouragement and opportunities you always offer me to make me shine.

Thank you a lot and God bless you all.

Dedication

My first dedication goes to my son and pride Nana Ato-Kwamena Akyer Brainoo and my godfather Emmanuel Boadi, Monitoring and Evaluation Specialist in UNDP.

Other dedication goes to my wonderful mother Nancy Nakuo Kumodzi also to Selorme Azumah (Ghana) for the opportunities given me in developing myself. I love you all.

1. What God Has Put Together

If we could press a button
And instantly be one through marriage
There will be no divorces
But that is not possible
Everything in life is a process
Actually, life is a process

It has joys, sorrows, ease and difficulties
Always know that marriage
Is not mans own idea
But the divine design
Originated in the heart of God

Vows do not supernaturally bring two together in
harmony
They are a promise from one person to the other
That they will not give up
If we constantly find fault with people, they become
discouraged and get worse and not better

Find the positive things in your marriage partner
And concentrate on them, leaving the rest to God

Know that you two can achieve your vision
Have a choice for your future
Let your first love be as
You first loved your Maker

2. The Race

As the saying goes
Quitters never win
Winners never quit
Running the race, is never easy

The period one starts crawling
Then it turns into walking
It doesn't end but jogging
Whereas it continuous in running
Strongly in flying
Then what else

As you start
You meet frown faces and disappointed ones
Also happy and courageous faces
The saying becomes easy
But the going gets tougher

Though it tarries
The vision and mission
Is to fulfil the work
It is never easy
But then, remember

'Never say, I am weak and tired to continue'

3. When Would Manna

I see them rushing to the temple
Only on these days do they show concern
Blind as I am
All seem dark to me
As I stand at the roadside
All these while, the sun scorches at me
It rains on me heavily

They pass by me, few gave me coins
Just from my abode is the worship place
I have stood for years¨
Nobody ever took me in to help me
I had longed to hear what they hear
And see what they are seeing
As I stood, all I hear are noises
Fill with joy of praises and worship
Why then should I be judged in my imagination?

But I thought in your presence
My thirst will be assuaged
And my dry leaves will be made green

But I am still the palm that I am
They shall surely be accounted to it

4. So It Saith

Sometimes I tend to forget
That he the immortal and invisible has promised.
Though it becomes difficult as life passes
We need to hold on to that last faith
Giving up on the way is easy
The moment I remember
The Holy Scroll:

'When you pass through the waters
I will be with you
And through the rivers
They will not overwhelm you
When you walk through the fire
You will not be burned or scorched
Nor will the flame kindle upon you'

That is what He says
Do you believe?
Will you believe?
I am waiting for mine to be fulfilled

5. Complains

How long will thy word come true?
For how long will man suffer?
It has not been easy for me
Am I Job to be considered?
They gathered lies against me
Together do they despise me

Nobody has ever congratulated me
Not even the little I do

Wonderful, this indeed is wonderful
After those years of tumult
I met a miracle
I give out cars as gifts
This is splendid

Of a truth, his word is true
'When it reads-
'For I will pour water upon him who is thirsty and
floods upon the dry grounds
I will pour My Spirit upon your offspring
And my blessing upon your descendants

His words are so true
Just lean on it

6. Can It Be

Can it be?
Can it come to pass?
Will it be accomplished?
What the Lord has said about me
Can it be fulfilled?

I sometimes get confuse
When I see his saying-
'I will go before you and level the mountains to make
the crooked places straight; I will break in pieces the
doors of bronze and cut asunder the bars of iron. And
I will give you the treasurers of darkness and hidden
riches of secret places, that you may know that it is
I, the Lord, the God of Israel, Who calls you by your
name'

Will it ever come to pass?
People give testimonies of him
Wretched as I am
Can His saying be real in my life?
I am of unclean lips
Full of iniquity
I wonder, can it be . . . .

7. I Saw Him

There is a man I know
Who is more than caring
He is more than I can love
He is real to me
I cannot explain how I met him

He delivered me from the pit of hell
He set me free from the fowler
He brought liberty to my soul

What a friend I can boast of
He is more than I can say
I have seen him
I have tried him
I have tested him

Who knows Him more than I?
He is my all in all
I will not forget him
Not even when I pass in sleep

In the unseen world
Will I glorify him
I have seen him

8. Love

Millions of millions tried to understand love
They have tried it
They have gone through it
But they never accomplished it

Love is patient, love suffereth long, love is kind, love
envieth not, love vaunteth not itself, love is not puffed
up, love doth not behave itself unseemly, love seeketh
not it own . . . .

Blessed are they that accomplish it
Moments turn bright and dark
How many do these in moments of darkness
Love is invisible to pretenders
But it is really visible to heartbeats

Love! I once wish to touch and feel

Whatever condition, whatever period
Love whispers 'When you pass through the roaring
waters and when you are ship wrecked I will be with
you

9. Learning To Love

We may be in love when we get married
Often it is more physical attraction than real love
Love is not a feeling
It is a decision to be committed
To an individual and to their happiness and well being
Love is not talking, it is always giving

When the emotional excitement is over
One must learn to love as God loves us

There is a treasure of good things inside each person
The love of God working through us
Is the key to unlocking that precious potential

People have to do a lot of hard work
To get them out
We must not abandon our hope
Before we receive the answer

Let us not be weary in well doing
For in due season we shall reap
If we faint not

Always remember
The end justifies the means

10. Focus

It's a challenge to change your focus in life
What you focus on
Makes you who you are
You focus makes you a master

Focus brings and makes you a master
This brings into you determination
After that, there is a vision
From there an activity
This resolves in a task
Also there comes a success
Successes are with rewards

You can only find this in God
That is why he focused, prepared, formed, fashioned
and created the universe

You can create a pleasant universe
Under this universe
Have a focus
God is the only ultimate goal
What you focus on today
Makes you what you are tomorrow

11. Something Good

Have faith for tomorrow
Faith must be your hope
Hope is the happy anticipation of something good
It is the powerful, spiritual force
That serves as a platform for one's faith

Hope is an attitude of looking, expecting and
believing while you wait
Learn to live like a little child with expectancy
Choose to put your confidence in God today
And stop wearing yourself out-

Change is in God

The power of hope
Is just in your heart
Something good is going to happen if you learn to lean

Lean on God
Your ultimate goal

12. Your Answer

God is a marvellous designer
He has made a dynamic device right under your nose
It holds the capacity of life and death
It can be used to verbalised God's word
Or to do the devil's dirty works

Is your speech hard, sharp and pressing?
Do you want to change your words?

Then learn to fellowship with the Lord
He will enable you to tame your tongue
And make every most of your word
That proceeds from your mouth

Bring your mouth into agreement with God
And begin to walk in victory

13. Restoration

This, they always say
Is to lead back, give back and to refresh
It is a movement back to the place of departure
Our God is in restoration

He restores our thinking, our ability to make good
decisions and our emotional ability
This brings us to full health

This is one of happiness, peace and hope
For the future
It is not a plan of misery, failure, poverty, sickness or
disease

The devil's aim is to sabotage God's plan
God desires to straighten out everything that was
damaged in our life
From the initial point of injury, forward

True restoration begins with recognising
What has produced the words in our soul?

14. Abusement

Sometimes we remember of how we were abused
Through verbal, physical, emotional and sexual means
We then suffer from thinking, decision making and
emotional pains
The more intense and prolonged the abuse
The more emotionally unstable we become

Stop talking bad about the persons who hurt you
Avoid rehearsing the injury you have received

Focus on something good about the person's character
Try to forgive, release and pray for those who hurt you

If we steadfast to forgive
God will heal our feelings
God will bring us to justice
It may take sometime
But he will honour his word

If we handle things his ways
Then he will pay as back

Not less than double for our trouble

Never meditate on how you were abuse

15. Bitter Fruits

Identifying problems brings victory
Many are filled with bitter hearts
Because they are confronted, confuse, dry,
disappointed or stopped
Anytime your heart is full of bitterness
You begin to hate who you are

No matter how challenging your situations may seem,
God stands ready with the remedy-
You shall not be put to shame
For you shall forget the shame of your youth
And you shall not seriously remember
The reproach of your widowhood anymore

Let's stop trying to remove the bad fruit
And deal with the root
We can experience freedom
From a shame-based nature

And the fruit it bears

16. Addiction

When we do not find fulfilment in relationships
We resort to seeking fulfilment
From a wide variety of things
Then addiction starts its journey
After one cannot bear living without it
When the devil starts its vices against us
We are addicted to
Worry, excessive, planning, reasoning, hoarding,
sleeping, eating and isolated

We need to transfer our confidence
And dependence unto God alone
With a personal relationship with him
We experience freedom and lasting satisfaction
He is the unchanging rock of our salvation

Even if all our other support systems fall apart
We will still be standing firm
If we are rooted and grounded in Christ

Do not be addicted to the self-desires

But unto Christ

17. It Endures Forever

God's mercy is new every morning
He never changes his mind
He still has the same great plan for our lives
We can receive all the love and acceptance
We lost in our childhood
And so do the scroll says

'The Lord is my shepherd, I shall not lack'

The moment the enemy hurts us, God stands a ready
with a plan of complete restoration for our lives.

If we will get alone with God
He will reveal his reasons for our present pains

Through Christ, we can discover the root
Of all our problems

And the God of peace
Shall let his Glory endure forever
In our lives

18. Alone With Christ

There are times when you are alone
In the moment of sadness
When all seems sorrow
Here comes a comforter
A hope to hopelessness

19. Lovingly

Lovingly has he enriched us with His Grace
It is the power and ability of God available
To meet our every need, without any cost

Receiving salvation-
Being fill with the Holy Spirit
Fellowshipping with God
And having victory in our daily lives

All these are based on Grace, which is loving.

'It is by free Grace that you are saved through faith.
And this is not of yourselves but it is gift of God

Whatsoever man cannot earn
God gives it out freely
By His loving Grace

Jesus became our substitute
Paying the debt, we owed
At no cost to us

20. Frustration

Most at times when new converts listen to the word
They are ignorant of the fact that is for them
Then the devil comes in to destroy it

You may seem to be trying
But all your efforts turns into frustration
Until you find the word which says
'All who depend on the law are under a curse and
doom for disappointment

Still it
People believed in their hearts that
'If I don't do this, God doesn't love me anymore
If I do not do that, I am going to lose my salvation

Many are destroyed
Because they do not know the truth

Let disappointment go
And your years will be full of joy

21. A Radical Freedom

The flesh wants to conquer its own problems
So it can get the glory
'God sets Himself against the proud and haughty
But gives grace continually to the lowly
Those who are humble enough to receive it

Give up labouring and start believing
Our faith is the channel
And his Grace is the power

Keep your eyes off methods
And focus on God
He will always be available to meet your need

Time is not spent for grace and freedom
It is a gift met for good works or for sale

The more time you spend with him
The more you learn to relax
And relate to God

A man's mind plans his way but the Lord directs his
steps and makes them sure
Anytime we are confuse
We get far from our planning

22. The Past

God's mercy and loving kindness
Are new every morning
He eagerly desires to do a new thing in your life
To bring you relief
And make a way
Where there seems to be no way
His gifts of a fresh start
Is available to you

Do not let the pain of the past
Hold you hostage
It is full of remorse
There is no appreciation in it
The memory of failures
Eat up all your good endeavours

Learn how to put it behind you
And press it to the promise
Of just a new beginning

Let God give you a new start

23. When Rejected

Rejection starts as a seed
The devil plants it into our lives
Through a variety of events, that takes place
At the earliest stages of our lives
His aim is to make us feel
Like we have no value and that, nobody wants us
'Know that he is a liar'

We are of great value

We are fearfully
And wonderfully made
Through the finished works of Christ
We can overcome rejection

Then there we shall surely
Experience the fullness of our inheritance

These are righteousness, peace
And joy in the Holy Spirit

You may feel self-centred in a circle of eyes
Always remember
Christ is with you

24. Are You Satisfy

Many things are what you desire
But the one thing, that is searched for
Is a great genuine of joy?
It is not found in the stuff we own
Alternatively, the situation we are in

When one depends on those
Life becomes a roller coaster of ride vicissitudes

Real joy is only experienced in the present of God
With him, the hope of glory in us
We have everything we need

'In his presence is fullness of joy, at his right hand,
there are pleasures forever'

As we seek God alone

You will discover

That in his presence alone

There is fullness of joy

25. This Is All

Giving is part of the character of God
Learning to receive begins with salvation

'A channel is an instrument or place where things
flow through which is always fresh, clean and pure'

Is God using you as a channel to bless life's?
God wants you to prosper spiritually, physically,
mentally, socially and financially

The flesh without the Spirit is greedy

The only way to experience a fresh flow of genuine joy
is to learn
To be a giver and not a taker

Do not be full of greediness

Do not be a reservoir

Be a channel of giving

26. Interaction

Are you satisfy
With the quality
Of your relationships
You may be different from other people

Everyone needs to be loved,
Understood
And appreciated
You must learn how to walk in love

When empowered by Christ

You can get your mind off
To yourself and unto others

When you are interacted with love

Your results are always
Surely amazing

27. Good As Best

A good marriage does not happen
It takes effort
To be successful in a relationship
Learn to give and not to get

God's desire is that
You enjoy each other

Have fun, laugh, and play
Have communion, pray
And enjoy all of life together

You can achieve
The marriage of your dreams

Through

The power of God

28. Desiring A Deep One

Are you dissatisfied?
Because you have not experience
The fulfilment of your desires
God is calling you to a deeper life

Do not let your mind get in the way
Go deeper than how you feel
What you want
And what you think

Exalt the word of God above your thoughts
Feelings
And desires

Experience a deeper
And more meaningful life

They that know their God
Shall be strong
And they shall do exploits

Desiring to dive deep
And even deeper

29. The Power

'Behold I have given you authority and power
To trample upon serpents and scorpions
And over all the power that the enemy possess
And nothing shall in any way harm you

The power of God is to restore
To mend
To give back stolen goods
To bring back to an original state
This is the desire of God

This is not always easy
It always takes time and patience
God has installed into his children
Authority and power over the enemy

That great, marvellous foundation is
To be in great obedience

God is ready, willing and able
Just to restore us

But we must remain faithful

30. The Key To It

Obedience is the key to taking back what the devil stole

It takes one to be in-
-Submitting to Gods authority
-Submitting to the constituted authority that God has placed over us
-Taking authority over ourselves
-Knowingly doing the will of God
-Standing on your ground to resist the devil

To win the battle is through persistence

If only we will not

. . . 'lose heart and grow weary and faint in acting noble and doing right . . . in due time and at the appointed season, we shall reap . . . if we do not loosen and relax our courage and faint . . ."

You can be who you are meant to be

God will give you
Double for your trouble

Eat It

If your heart desire is to come higher
Then walk with God in love
Allow yourself to be ushered into the very throne
room of God

The perfect sacrifice of Jesus blood-
Provided cleansing power as well as overcoming
power

Love the word, study the word, and sing about the
word
Be transformed by the word
The word of God is a mighty—
Two edged sword against the enemy
That can bring healing and transformation to you

As you put this and make this
A practical principal to work in your life

You will also discover the power
You need to claim your victory

It Is Real

Life is not always the picture that we know
It has its failures and achievements
No one understands how really it is like
It is full of mysteries
If one will just be connected to God
Have a close relationship with him
Than his memory shall just be master minded
To see the realities of his glory
All that we need to do
Is to take a step
Have a firm decision and aspiration

Though we must be concerned for both
Natural and physical necessities
Christ must be our ultimate goal

Have you ever seen one in love with God?
Just like Benny Hinn, Kathryn Kuhlman, Patrick
Hagan, Joyce Meyer, and Rebecca Brown and so on

Just try God and test him
Your life will be a surprise to you

You will never remain the same

Covetous

Stop getting jealous on what people have
Just sit down and concentrate
Begin to use what you have
Some people do not have joy over their life
Just stop thinking of what you cannot do
Think of what you can do

Focus on what you have
And God will bless you
Lock the room of self-pity
Throw the key into the very deep

Never be a self—centred woman
Nor a self-centred selfish man

This is the time to dream higher
Be at peace with all men

The spouting glory of the most one
Shall surely be seen
Focus on what you have

Just do not be covetous

Greatness

Every great desire comes from
A very great person
False comfort destroys our priority
Greatness is sought for

Ordinary people are useless to every prudent person
A great person is of whom people benefit from

'I haven't decided is a failure of the flesh
As a seed you must fall . . . . humility
Die . . . . give up external features
Rot . . . . accept social ridicule
Mix with the soil . . . . life
Re germinate . . . new vision

Greatness is a decision
Go out for it
You must pay the cost
You will achieve it

Move out of the comfort zone
To the zone of unpleasantly to man

Let your life expose and be important

And needed with all cost to people

You have to give up better things of the flesh before
you can attain greater things in the spiritual

What you hold must be prune and your life will be
fruitful
Nobody wins without overcoming challenges
What we gain out of our tongues speaking makes us
great, excellent and of quality

The greatness of a man is paid through a price and
aspirations
If you want to win, do something new
Nobody will make you great if you do not come out
great

Something in the inside
Must surely motivate the outside

Try This

There are conditions
When one holds
A strong accusation against another one

Why do these happen?

He will reply-
My precious possession was snatch from one through
the gospel

Bitterness and hurt fills the person's heart
Then there is a problem of unforgiveness

He says—
Why should I create a successful way for him to
demonstrate and succeed?

But you know
I understand your emotions
Try to forgive, just as Christ forgives you

Was all the bitterness from your heart?

Christ will just offer you something great and
immeasurable

There Is

I Know I am at fault
There is something wrong somewhere
My life has been one of unconsciousness

God why don't you just explain all to me
Anytime I remember my past and present
I still feel that guiltiness
I did a mistake
Why couldn't I tame my tongue?

I am guilty conscious
My sin is more than I can carry
I would love to be alone
And alone with the Holy Spirit

I want to desert from the ridicule of men

I know there is some wrong somewhere
I wish a love one will just reveal
All the bad I have done to me to know

There is something wrong somewhere
Who will help me out

I need someone badly

Because there is something, wrong

Hold on my dear
Did you hear that voice?
That small still voice

-My child, thou should stop thy worry,
If I the father have forgiven you, then worry not of
your past anymore
The blood has cleanse them all
Just think of today and tomorrow
Do not allow yesterday's misfortunate issues to tie
you down
Else, you will never grow

What Beauty

I do not know the perfect beauty in me
I was really close to these seven stars
They enjoyed the company
Each had a behaviour I hated
So I discuss each with the contrary

Until I realised their heart
The four stars fled away fearfully
Two stars rose against one star strongly

The one star was my heart and the heart of the maker
But I kept asking my maker
Why me . . . why not anyone else

Why is it that God sometimes leave his children to
face the battle alone
Then there arise mistakes, failures and no
achievement

Still the two who do not know each other are against
that star in my heart

God are you still saying you have not seen anything

Astray

I had to lead astray
A whole lot of sheep
I was filled with great fear and agony

But then
Nobody was comforting my wounded heart so I lead
them all astray

Some went back into the mud
Others struggled to clime the weak and shaky ladder
rejected

My wounds increase day in and day out
Who is ready to swallow my words?
Why I pour them out

Who is ready to swallow my wounds?
When I pour them out

I sometimes become afraid of the fact that on the
judgement day
Will He query me of this great shame?

I will have wished to come into another world to re
start my duty than to be in Hades

But this can never be done
It is really a remorse for me
When I turn their chains into captivity

-then in the dream I saw Him walk to me,
My daughter, thou art free, thy sins I have washed
away
You are free, remember them no more-

Another One More

God I need another chance
Just one more opportunity
It was all mistakes

But I know and always comforts myself
That every problem has its own benefits
Every situation changes your position
Problems brings awareness
Mistakes brings carefulness
Failures make you think again

Giving up brings an unsearchable information

All these results in setting up a goal
I need another opportunity God
Please allow me for the second time

I do not want to give up anymore
I will not focus anymore on my mistakes

I believe this is the time to look back into my
achievements
And do better

Please another chance

The Summer Harmattan

Anytime I come out of His presence
Then I see the broken arrow
In his heart

I am forced to let him know my reason of not
rejecting him and travelling away from his abode

It becomes hectic for me
I become more
Of a dump object
When and after he leaves
Then his eagerness is strengthen

Who will volunteer?
Just to be my mouthpiece

God the father has done his part
Christ has accomplish his part
The Holy Spirit is still hovering around
Waiting just for me

If I take the initiative
He will help me right there
All I need is someone to help me

Break the chains that have put my mouth together

Can You

It is incredible at times
It is inexplicable
When in the midst of the so called
Children of the great Jehovah

Look down on you
All shun away from you
Because you were ignorant of your mistakes

No one comes out to help you out
But they assume you know
After the mess up
They shun from you

It is not easy standing this
Can you bear the ocean of tears?
In people hearts when they are shun
I can stand in the shoes of all

All move together in love
But you are being rejected on the way
What actually is the mistake you have done that
nobody has ever done?

Thy Presence

Thy presence is full of joy
That I cannot tell

I just cannot live anymore that past life
It is incredible having understanding in thee

Not until that day
I put my trust and hope in man
I depended on man
I relied on and adhered to 'woman'

It has been of uncertainty
She then told me
I am not sure of myself for you

Gracious!
I have been waiting my days on you
I have been wasting my times on you

Is better I forget about woman again
It is really a lesson that I have learnt

Heaven helps me not to repeat this mistake

Never will I repeat it again

I promise to advice all
To put their trust in God only, yes only
Man will always let you down

Part B

Poems on Emancipation and Educational issues

Is There Hope

Lest we should be killed
Before the armed men
Blood gushed out from their nostrils
Victims laid half dead on the street
The children screamed and yelled for help
These people have come again

They put us into slavery
Just in the name of Christianity
Where are our good, our precious diamonds
They troubled our lonely souls
We were put in chains
Chains heavier than weapons

Many were slaughtered
And many were hanged
The women wept
But the sorrows of them were not considered
They teach love but practice wickedness

We had our way of living
We were in harmony
We were in happy moments

But when they came
They split our unity
They took our beautiful women
They took all our expensive and valuable resources

Here are they—back again
In the name of bringing independence

I have had no hope
The day drew nigh for my execution
I will soon . . . .
Soon see and join the bones of loved ones

What will be my final recitation?
My final prayer-
I was about to when they . . . .
Oh blood, I see it

Still It

We came all the way from Congo, to go to our
promised land
Eve's were carrying infants at their back
Those who will soon be in labour were amongst us
The strong carried our goods
Our four legged animals were indeed tired
But because of their god given ability and talent
They ignored thirst and hunger

We reached the desolate land
No living being we found there
All we heard of is the wind whistling
Many could not hold their breath
Uncountable died on the way
We dared not care for them
All was their struggling for the sake of individuality
and God for oneself

Water could be stored their adam's apple
What a moment of sorrow and pain
Some secretly fed on their young ones

The number decreased as we were approaching our
promised land
Millions turned into thousands
Thousands into hundreds
Then hundreds into tens

We jumped with joy
Though weak but run happily
We came, we saw it
We stepped there, we saw the land
We aboded there

But poor us
Can riches bring happiness
We are now eight to enjoy life"
The dual women wept as they sat down

It was tears of joy

Those moments are passed and gone

That's forever

But if it might come again . . . .

Critics

The universe is full of critics
Man has never done anything to be appreciated
Voices have even criticised the real creator

They proclaim-
The universe came on its own
If there be any strong spiritual being
'Why then all my suffering'

When you try making a goal
They continue criticising
As you climb the ladder
The same people try hard to pull you down

Then they later, criticise you of laziness
Man ! Oh man ! Man criticises!

You suffer on your own
When you make it, when you finally achieve it
There is a long queue at your door
They begin to cry for assistance
They pretend to love you and show concern

Trials begin to rise
Poverty, pestilence, famine and all rises again
Those who have been established well through you—all
desert you
They begin to criticise you again
They say-

'He was once rich, he was arrogant
Now dry leaves have gathered round him
Let's depart, he can help himself'

It is not all,
'L'argent n'est fait pas le bonheaur'

Opportunities open again
Happiness, joy and riches
Comes in abundance than before,

Here they come again
More than ever before
Where are my weapons

As red eyed as I am
I will just . . . .

Women

We are proud to be women of this age
We believe we are unique
We are special and nothing else

Why continue to degrade and humiliate us
Always we hear what you say—
'Was is not woman who started sin?
Didn't she force man to take the apple?
'Was it not woman who made him to be killed? She
persuaded him, His eyes were plugged off. His hair
was shaved off"

Was it not woman
'Was it not woman who was bathing on top of the
building and tempted him
This made him conspired against the husband to be
killed at the battle front

Have you forgotten so soon
Who bears the baby for forty four weeks
Who labours for the child
Who cleanses all filthy things
Who cleans the bath house, the kitchen and so on. Who
cooks the various food
Who creates opportunities for the brother to be educated

Remember we are now at the position of being at the same seat with you
Not to forget, who breastfeeds the baby

Have you forgotten so soon
We are surprise
Was it not Dorcas who was generous
Wasn't she the one who resurrected again because of giving
Was it not Deborah who led the bath with Barak
Wasn't her and Jael that God placed his glory
Was it not Esther who found favour before the Kind and his whole counsel

If it had not been her, Modecai and all the Jews would have been killed
Was it not Mary who gave birth to the saviour

It is enough, Stop condemning us
We have made it
And will surely do more

Days Of Past

As I rest in the wheel chair
Sad as I am
Looking so desperate

My dreams have torn apart
I looked at the images on the papers
He was once strong
He had all the abilities
Then I said, there are more days to come
I will still wait

Many cherished my visions
They followed me to hear more
Then one said,' If you will only put these dreams into
action, many bees and flies will admire you
My dreams and aspirations kept on increasing from
day to day

I still continued my song-
There are more days ahead for preparation

I run errands here and there
Always looking busy
I was always on the go

But then I was supporting many to attain theirs

They even isolate from me saying-
You can also do it, don't be greedy
I laughed over it

Now dreams came into memory
I listed them down in big books
It was almost full up everywhere

People said'-
We need that and that information, when will you
publicise it
I still sang: 'I have more days ahead of me

Never did I know this would be
'I was on an errand when a vehicle knocked me down.
The specialist said, 'You have got a problem with
your memories and you will not be able to remember
anything again'

People came rushing taking some of my books but I
could not remember exactly the information inside
them
Never did they return again
If I had know . . .

Any Problem

They claim—I had a problem
But I never got to know of it
Children gather to look at me when I pass by
They laugh happily, as they watch
But as soon as I draw nigh, they panic
And run with terror in their faces

Do I have a problem
I know I am the healthiest person
I sleep at the pleasant places
I eat the most enjoyable food
I drink hygienic water

But when they sleep at where I sleep, mosquitoes bit
them and they are infected with fever
When they eat the food I enjoy they get running
stomach. When they are about to drink the water that
I drink they frown and say it smells so they throw it
away

I know that I am neat and healthy
For years now
I have never been injected
Or never have I been given any pill

I am always happy and talk to my invisible friends
I am the happiest being

You see . . . . I don't have any problem

I had always long to tell them of the invisible beings I
see and talk to, but they run away

Some hold their nose when I pass by

I know my problem
I easily get annoyed when someone watches me too
much, because they want to take my possessions
that I carry with me everywhere. Because of this,
I sometimes chase them or beat them or spit on the
floor. This all my problem.

But they still claimed that
I have a problem

Since all run when they see me
Who then is the problem
They have a big problem . . . .

Law

I was already existing when it came
I am respected in my small-scale village
They attend to my commands

Then one day, all I hear was-
These have all come to an end
We have our written norms to guide us
This is corrupt ! Totally corrupt

I never entered into a classroom
I neither held a chalk nor a pen
My wisdom was in my brains

I was born with it
I acquired the know how
And I gained understanding

My years are far from theirs
How can I be moved to the command of a book
Should I obey an inanimate object

Not I ! Not me either!
The gods are there
My ancestors are there

They have been in existence from ancient times and
until now

I came to where they call, 'The City'
I studied how to control the object that allows
movement on the street with the four legs

I saw many stopping at a place
So I asked one, Why the stopping
Then he said,' These is not yet green'
Damn it ! Should I obey that thing there. Am I not
superior than that
How can I obey an object. Damn it

I passed by the cars and when . . . .
All of a sudden, another four wheel came from
another direction then bang ! to my four leg object.
Fortunately he was more injured than I was

My eyes went dark and my arms were amputated
Now here am I sitting in the dark place in this prison
All I feel is unbearable beatings and insults from
different corners

A Lesson Of Cause

I have always dreamed of it
People went there and came
They sat in flashy cars
I saw ear rings pieced in their tongues, nose and so on

They were just spending money in town
I told myself
I will also be there

Mum and dad offered me money for my final
entrance fee. It was quiet huge
Without their consent, I went away
As the bird moves in the sky, I promised myself, I
would also come back in a flashy car

We reached the land, but I forgot
Who am I going to stay with
People came to embrace their love ones
But here I was
Immediately, I became sad
Then I gathered momentum and said
I am also there, I will go back with a flashy car
Oh What is happening to me
I was shaking furiously

This is not the weather I am acquainted with

I saw white sand and balls raining, I was freezing so I
dashed for a cover
Then I run into some people smoking and sniffing
something

I sat two miles away from them just admiring from afar
The light of cars approached nearer
I stood up and thanked my stars

They all run away seeing the cars
I stood up waiting

They suddenly shouted at me
'You are under arrest for smoking
Haven't we warned you of drugs'?

I had wanted to explain my situation
But all that came from my mouth was
Messy constructional sentences
The next day I was deported

Now here I am with all bees saying
Shame unto you

Memories

There have been moments, conditions and period
When one have to be in a memory

There have been centuries, decades, years, months,
weeks, days hours, minutes and seconds when one
have to remember the past

A rich man is put into miseries
And a poor man also into miseries
The past never leaves the mind

The mind is greater and have more capacity than the
computer or the internet

When one plays around, when you jump around when
you make jokes together, you are never taken into the
past

The moments you sit alone
The moment everything is quiet and mild
The past just climbs into your memory

Days of bitterness
Of long suffering
Of pains and sorrow

Of unforgiveness
Then
Of joy
Of great achievements
They all creep into your mind

These are the moments you remember all your
mistakes, failures and shortcomings

Memories are always memories
When at all will one just forget memories

Sometimes it makes you sad, it makes you lose hope
Sometimes it makes you happy, you are filled with
determination

Memories
They are all memories

—

Dont Give Up

Sometimes in our life we all have pains, sorrows, and
bitterness and get troubled
When all friends have neglected you
When all relations have left you behind
When all turns to say,' You are a failure'
When all despise you
When all just look at you wrongly and begin to
criticise any effort you make
When all turn to say, 'You are wasting your time'

Never give up
Never say die
Never say I have thrown in the towel

It is still not too late
You can achieve a great thing in a moment
You can do it
Great men have achieve it

Abraham Lincoln struggled for the seat many times
before he attained it
Dr Kwame Nkrumah struggled to gain independence
for Ghana
Madela have to struggle for South Africa

Marcus Garbey once said,' The best and ever thing to
be is to be yourself'

You can make it
Be yourself and try harder
Just believe in yourself, have hope
You can make it

Remembering the past will pull you down
Just focus on the future

You have more days of preparations

Don't give up so soon ¨
Little by little, you can make it

Just make an effort
You can achieve your dreams and your goal

Try it ! Try hard ! You can do it

Lonely

There are moments when it seems nobody is caring
And you sit lonely at your abode
When all seems bleak

Where you hear of only the birds singing

All is quiet and lonely

Is there hope here
No one is passing by

Not a soul to be seen

This makes me think

I do think . . . .

This is really casual

I need someone to be close to

Oh life

Life

Everybody has his definition for it
Some says it is enjoyment
Others say it is a remorse
Who then qualifies to give it a name

It is not always the same
As we imagine and think
It is full of mysteries

Everyone is filled with a particular desire
They define lie in their own way
But truly it is not always the same

.

Forget about critics, failures and seems
Just remember that the maker is always there
Man have its own way of living
Animal have its own way of living
Spiritualism has its own way of living

Remember that is all, all about life
Who can give us a great definition
Just for life
Life is a mystery
Indeed is inexplicable

So They Say

It is surprising and hectic
When you hear them saying
'We are a people of democratic powers
No one can infringe on any one's right
You have the free will to be in a suitable political
party
You have the right to vote'

So I imagine and ask myself does this really operate
Numerous are ignorant of their rights
Still they believe they are democratic
Millions are ignorant of their liberty¨
And still kowtow to the wishes of men
Do you call this democratic

Slavery is still in existence
Not between colours and differences
But then-
Among the identical family
Do you call this democracy

Someone need to explain again
What actually it is

The PHD

Some are born to progress
Others are born to suffer
Is the order of the tongue

This is never true
Becoming who you want to be is a decision,
perseverance, commitment and gaining

Whilst the secessionist endeavour to make but gives
up
Some seriously sit, plan and 'Pull Him Down'
It the nation is not developed, it means that, it is the
attitude of the citizens

Instead of barking and supporting each other
The same voices who say 'We need development are
the same people who say :
Why should I sit for him to prosper
I will go heaven and earth for us to be at the same
level and at the appropriate time, I will flourish'

Africa

That was the name given to it
A—Alienated from many where they are a minority
F—Freedom is their passion as their hearts cry out
R—Revolution is their hearts cry as they long for
change
I—Injustice, their daily battle as they are confronted
unequally
C—Calamity becomes their daily bread out of war and
so on
A—Abolition, they cry out to those that consider them
as nothing

Why, why, why are the many questions they have no
answers for?
Do we look too different from them?
Do we act too weird than them`?
What common have we with animals that we are
tainted?

There they go again as they meet many of our kinds

Do you have planes in your country?
Do you have buildings in your country?
Do you have tigers or lions as your pet in your country?
And many more

This breaks the heart of many when asked
We are of different origins but one people
We are of different colours but with same mind
We are of different development but have common
things

This is our heart cry
Nigger is not our titles
Nigger is not a soft word
Nigger is highly offensive

Nigger was used for black slaves and that is to be no
more
But it is sad, how many of us even know the meaning
Seeing many of us even using Nigger amongst
ourselves
How will others change their mind?

My people lets arise and change to be known on better
terms
This is the time to arise, be one and change for change
has come

Freedom

Freedom Freedom Freedom Freedom Freedom
That is their cry as they keep crying aloud
'Put in chains
Being wiped with heavy robs
Being pulled on the ground as their skinned tears out
Being spat at with no pity
Being punished for what they know nothing of . . .'

That did not stop their mouths and hearts from
crying aloud
Freedom Freedom Freedom Freedom Freedom
They cried and yelled their last breaths with vigour
and pain
They screamed their request out from throats of thirst
They screamed as loud as they can, though their
voices were tired

Freedom Freedom Freedom Freedom Freedom
The babes were taken from the women that laboured
them forth
The babes cried like the bats of the nights
Whence they were taken, their mothers knew not

They were beaten with irons heavier than they could
be carried
They were beaten with rods heated so hard
They were beaten with canes that brought sore
They were beaten with weapons of pain and deaf

In the sand they were pulled with no passion
They were dragged so hard as if they had no life
They were dragged as though they had no souls
They were dragged as though their spirits were dead
But as they were dragged on those heavy floors
On those floors with gravels, stones, broken glasses,
termites and so on
Their souls, their spirits screamed with pain to see
their body toil

As I walked to the front of the warriors to beg of their
mercy
I fell on my knee and screamed with anger, pain, and
bitterness
I screamed and my heart jumped out of my body and
went far away
My soul departed from me and my body cried to
make it come
Why, why, the battle was led by our own, one colour,
one origin . . .

Coloured Chalk

Molato Molato Molato Molato
That was the new slogan for them because they were
of mix race
Who ever knew there could be such a thing
If anyone told our fore fore grandfathers it will have
been a taboo
A taboo never to be spoken of
A taboo that will be seen as a silent pistol to kill the mass

How beautiful it looks when all can become one
How beautiful it looks when one can be with another
elsewhere
How pleasant it looks to see new souls of mix colours
How beautiful it looks to see them looking like both
parents
How beautiful it looks to see three different colours

Who knew he could have been the president

From amongst a home of different colours he was
originated
But today he became of a great leader for many
If our forefathers were told of this to come,
The seer will have been persecuted and executed

Amongst all the smiles from many as these changes
goes on
There are still questions unanswered
Many still believe, Molatos are worse than niggers

What is their sin to be troubled of when they are
innocent?
What trouble have they caused to be titled as such?
What pain have they caused people to be isolated
How could they fall victims of lovers who brought
them forth

Awkward as it looks today
Tomorrow will tell of a different story
When flood comes, the fishes eat the ants
When the water dries, the ants eat the Fish
Surprising as each one gets its turn
So shall all these never exist one day to come
Where colour, language, status and so on will never be
notified
Because evolution will be, complete for nature to smile

Green Pastures

That was their names: sojourners
That was their names: hustlers

That was their names : travellers
That was their names : refuge seekers

That was their names: immigrants
That was their names : asylum seekers

They came from afar and beyond
All for one purpose
They struggled their ways through, as they were
determined
Hope and restoration was their hopes as they fought
with aims

How they will survive, was a question for many
But risky as it seem they were ready to take risks and
have remedies
Discriminated and treated unjustly but they weary
not their hearts

In their own homes, they found love and happiness
In their own homes, joy was not to be sought for

But in the land so strange to them with little or no
acceptance
In the land so strange to them with little or no love
In the land so strange to them with hate and fear
They still were determine to settle through as many
more migrate

Education is what many sought for because little can
be done
Shelter becomes a challenge but they get their abodes
like a bird
Great and equal they desire to be, but of no welcome
they are given
Of same value, they get themselves educated but it
still becomes same

Discrimination cannot be ended
Fearful and in tolerated as it seemeth
Many still crossed their fingers with high hopes
That one day things will change for them to be given
same chances

Africa they shout to the many; Lets unite in the land
we are feared

The Unending Slavery

The women screamed, yelled & wept for help, as their
infants struggled to sleep for a minute behind their
back
Clothed partly with shame with no words to defend
their innocence, all they could do was to walk on with
pain

Those chains, were heavy, heavier than weapons as
their feet wearied to moved
Their men were stroked at different paces no matter
how much they fell on their feet.
Freedom, freedom, freedom was all their words no
matter the strokes they took

Alas, the centuries changed, many found themselves
on those strange lands
Without chains, without strokes, but still that freedom
they fought never came
When will it end, when will the story end, when will it
be a fairy, the answer, no one knows of . . . .

Your Personal / Diary pages

Your Personal / Diary pages

Other Books written by the Author

The Mysteries of a Virgin's Agony
(Love stories put into poetry)

About the Author

She is multi—talented and does best what she loves doing. She is a passionate woman who has the flair of putting what she sees, feels and experiences, hears and understands in the form of poetry in a very way that appeals to the senses of the audience in a passionate and natural manner. Poetry has been her passion and life from her early teens. Cecilia Naa densua Quarshie is very articulate, creative and a good team player as well as a good motivator.

She has worked with different International Organizations such as the Planned Parenthood Association of Ghana, African Youth Alliance, Pathfinder International, Christian Health Association of Ghana, Academy for Education and Development, Travel & tours and many others for 7 years in Ghana before relocating to Finland to further her studies. She has worked in the areas of a Research Assistant, Counsellor, Ticket Sales Assistant, Peer Educator, Secretary and a Public speaker. She as well served on a number of Advisory boards in different Organisations both local and International. In some cases represented females and the youth in both local and International conferences and workshops.

In Finland, she has a hobby job apart from her normal work as a Performance Poet & a Singer. It is her passionate wish that readers enjoy reading her poems and relate it to real life situations.